WHERE ARE WE
Heading To?

WHERE ARE WE
Heading To?

THUSO KEWANA

THE REGENCY
PUBLISHERS

ISBN: 978-1-958517-13-0   (PB)
ISBN: 978-1-958517-12-3   (E-book)

Book Ordering Information

The Regency Publishers, International
7 Bell Yard London WO2A2JR

info@theregencypublishers.com
www.theregencypublishers.international
+44 20 8133 0466

Printed in the United States of America

Table of Contents

I dedicate this book to my beloved and dear mother, Koko Kate Kewana, whose spirit left this world in 1987 to the place of resting peace. She taught me from childhood how to fear and honour God. She was instrumental in my knowing God from childhood. It is through her discipline that today I am the man I am and the person I am. I will always be grateful to her for the education that she gave me.

May your soul rest in peace, Mvulane, Ncilashe.

I will always love you.

Acknowledgement

This is my first book. The writing of this book was possible because of my beloved wife Matshele Kewana, who was the source of encouragement every time I felt discouraged. She also played a major role in supporting me with prayer. I will always be indebted to my son Nceba, my daughters, Pitsi and Babalwa, and my adoptive son, Dakalo. They all played a role in motivating me to complete this book. I also extend my gratitude to my fellow congregants at Heart to Heart Ministries for their continuous prayers. I shared most of what is written here with them during our Sunday meetings.

I am grateful to my friend, Mzukisi Madikane, for persuading me not to give up on the truth. Thank you.

Thank you, Lebowa Malaka, for writing the foreword of this book. You are a friend indeed. May God bless you.

Foreword

I must acknowledge the commendable work that Thuso has done in this book, but even more I must express my respect for the courage he needed to capture this revelation of knowledge and defy his doubts, which arose from the fear of criticism. When I first read this book, I was shattered for a moment because I was also used to the very church system described in the book, and I must say that I was immediately struck by anxiety and doubt. Just like everybody else who will read this book, you may experience an inner commotion when you read the first few pages of the book, but I must reassure you that this is normal—especially when you've been at the centre of the church systems described in this book. When I read deeper and deeper, God started to give me a revelation. He told me to read with understanding and wisdom, and the whole book became a light to me.

This book has opened my eyes, and now I know my position in the church. I remember that the church is not the building in which we have fellowship but rather the people themselves. Every single page of this book focuses not on condemning people, but on the systems being applied in churches by some pastors (of course, not all). I now know that I should not operate on the themes of inferiority and condemnation that are preached in some churches. It's not the amount of material things I commit to God that will turn God's heart towards me. No, God's heart is already with me, and His love does not depend on how much I love or give Him. He loves me anyway, because He made me righteous. A word of caution: this book is not meant to divide churches, but rather to ignite dialogue in churches so that people may start reasoning together about their church systems in comparison to the heavenly systems that are God approved and ordained.

My believe is, yes, indeed, pastors are supposed to be God's mouth and feet for delivering God's word to the people. I believe that the church should take care of them, but I also believe that pastors should not impose their greediness on their congregations and rob their churches either by daylight or by night. As God said in His Word: **'My people perish from a lack of knowledge'** *(Hosea 4:6)*. This book is one other source that will fill you with some of that knowledge that you require to avoid perishing. Remember again that our pastors are gifts from God; that's why God says in His Word, **'I will give you pastors according to mine heart, which shall feed you with knowledge and understanding'** *(Jeremiah 3: 15, KJV, Cambridge edition)*. And so we still need to take care of them but, as I said earlier, in a God-approved and ordained manner.

Read and apply the revelation of this book in your church and you will be amazed how you will provoke heaven to pour out favour, blessings, and the love of God upon you, your church, and your families.

God bless you.

Malaka Lebowa

"Come now, and let us reason together",
says the Lord *(Isaiah 1: 18).*

Introduction

I have seen many negative situations unfold in churches today, all over the world, and especially in my country of South Africa. People are leaving churches. Some practice fellowship in their homes, but some leave the church and go back to their old lifestyles. Some leave to stay at home doing nothing.

This is because of the disappointments people experience with churches and church leadership. This is more prevalent with so-called spirit-filled or charismatic churches. The greed for worldly wealth, huge church membership numbers, and fame form the cornerstone of such dissatisfaction engulfing the congregants and encouraging them to leave the church of God. Pastors are involved in all sorts of ungodly behaviours.

It took a lot of courage and strength for me to start writing this book. I have prayed to God several times for guidance. I needed to understand if I should really do this. I guess in the absence of truth, evil thrives. I had two options. The first was to listen to the Holy Spirit and write a book that reveals the truth—a truth that would probably offend much of mankind and make myself unpopular with the world. The second was to please mankind by not revealing the truth, hiding the hypocrisies of the church, and facing the wrath of God. I know a lot of pastors will not be happy with what is written in this book, but it is not for me to please mankind and hurt God. I would rather be unpopular with men and please God than be popular with men at God's expense.

What is written in the book is what most of us are hearing at church, over the radio, and on television. One young man asked me if would not be better for a Christian not to hang the church's dirty linen before the public eyes of this world! My response was that, in the absence of truth, people begin to believe in lies, so we have to tell people the truth. It might hurt, but it is therapeutic and it will save a lot of lives. The devil is the father of lies, and the truth comes from God.

My only request of my readers is to please read my words with reason and an open mind. Question my thoughts and go to the scriptures to find answers. After all, the Word of God speaks for itself, and it will speak to you as well. Please do ask for the revelation from the Holy Spirit before you embark on reading this book. The book is going to challenge what you have heard and believed in from churches and pastors you have been involved with, which is sometimes a distortion of the Word of God. The truth is that the Word of God will always prevail over the lies of men.

Congregants must learn one thing—they must question ideas, not only outside the church but in the church also. People must not accept everything that is taught by their pastors and assume all their messages are scriptural. In Heart To Heart Ministries I always tell people that God challenges us to reason with Him. When the pastor is preaching in church, teach yourself to reason with him. He is a human being like you. If you can reason with your friends, what stops you then from reasoning with and questioning the pastor in church? I am sure this book will make you think twice.

I am not promoting radicalism in the church, but rather sanity and the voice of reason. The word of God is not for profit—not to anybody.

Where Are We Heading?

In late 1999 and early 2000 there was an overwhelming wave of a new type of preaching that rocked the church as a whole. This was started in United States by some pastors, and became known as 'prosperity gospel'. The obvious intention of this gospel was for the preachers to amass wealth and riches from their congregants and others to whom they preached. This indeed made them rich, and they continued to accumulate a lot of material wealth from their innocently unaware congregants. This sort of preaching also encouraged the congregation to see God as the material provider and hence to continue to seek him from this angle of Christianity. People began to look upon God as the Father who can gush out money overnight, provide for them, and solve all their material problems on the same day. All of a sudden, the love for God became conditional; believers would love Him provided He would meet their requirements in the way of material resources. The bible says, **'But seek first the kingdom of God and His righteousness, and all these things shall be added to you'** *(Matthew 6:33)*. Coincidentally enough this prosperity gospel was encouraging the congregation to give offering and tithing to the church so that they can get God's blessing. The strange thing is that pastor who preach about the material prosperity had more than anybody else in church. I remember one day I was watching one pastor preaching and he was talking about his new private jet and showed the congregation the fleet of cars that were parked in his yard. This is not what Christ encouraged:

> [16] Now behold, one came and said to Him, 'Good Teacher, what good thing shall I do that I may have eternal life?"
>
> [17] So He said to him, Why do you call Me good?. No one is good but One, that is, God. But if you want to enter into life, keep the commandments.'
>
> [18] He said to Him, 'Which ones?
> Jesus said 'You shall not murder,' 'You shall not commit adultery,' 'You shall not steal,' 'You shall not bear false witness,'
>
> [19] 'Honor your father and your mother,' and 'You shall love your neighbour as yourself'
>
> [20] The young man said to Him, 'All these things I have kept from my youth. What do I still lack?'
>
> [21] Jesus said to him, 'If you want to be perfect, go, sell what you have and give to the poor, and you will have treasure in heaven; and come, follow Me.'
>
> [22] But when the young man heard that saying, he went away sorrowful, for he had great possessions.
>
> [23] Then Jesus said to His disciples, 'Assuredly, I say to you that it is hard for a rich man to enter the kingdom of heaven' *(Matthew 19:16-23)*.

Verse 22 tells us that this young man was rich with worldly material possessions. The young man knew the Ten Commandments and kept them well. But it was not the Ten Commandments that were close to this man's heart, but rather his worldly wealth. Jesus was not saying to this young man that he must take what he had and donate to His ministry so that the ministry could give to the poor. He said 'give to the poor', meaning that the young man himself must take whatever he had and give it to the poor. Most pastors today would say you must give to their ministry or the church, not directly to the poor or to any other church but to the one where they preach.

One day I was talking to a rich man about God. He said to me, 'Thuso, I am very rich; what do I need God for? God is for poor people.' I asked him if he ever thought of giving to the poor. He said he had worked hard to accumulate whatever he had and thought everybody could do the same. He did not see a need to give lazy people what he had worked hard for. Earthly riches make people arrogant. I guess Solomon was correct when he said:

> **7 Two things I request of You**
> **(Deprive me not before I die):**
>
> **8 Remove falsehood and lies far from me; Give me neither**
> **poverty nor riches—**
> **Feed me with the food allotted to me;**
>
> **9 Lest I be full and deny You,**
> **And say, 'Who is the Lord?'**
> **Or less I be poor and steal,**
> **And profane the name of my God**
> *(Proverbs 30: 7-9).*

The world today is too materialistic. Pastors are competing over numbers of congregants in the churches of God, and this is about material wealth. Pastors today will do anything to lure rich people to the church they are leading. Tithing and offering are addressed through special sermons in churches today. Rich people and influential politicians get front seats and prominent positions in the church; they are kept closer to the pastor than anybody else. Poor people are kept far from the pastor and are not allowed to see the pastor without an appointment. Rich people and politicians do not need an appointment to see the pastor.

Pastors would rather profane the name of God by preaching about the importance of accumulation of worldly wealth than by preaching the truth of the gospel. The sermon about sowing to the church in order to receive a hundredfold like Isaac, and similar sermons about giving to the church are very common amongst pastors today. Sermons about God giving back more than what one has sown or given to the church are the daily bread in churches today. The truth, conditions, and the background about the verses used in the sermons are never explained to the people.

Material wealth belongs in this world. It is loved by the devil. After fasting for forty nights, Jesus Christ was tempted by the devil. One of the things the devil used to test Jesus was wealth. After the devil took Jesus up on a high mountaintop and showed Jesus all the kingdoms of the world he said to Jesus,

> **⁶ And the devil said to Him "'All this authority I will give You, and their glory; for this has been delivered to me, and I give it to whomever I wish.**
>
> **⁷ Therefore, if You will worship before me, all will be Yours.'**
>
> **⁸ And Jesus answered and said to him, 'Get behind Me, Satan! For it is written, "You shall worship the Lord your God, and Him only you shall serve"** *(Luke 4:6-8).*

Christ did not dispute what the devil was saying about possessing the authority and the glory of this world, but He rebuked the devil for wanting Him (Christ) to worship before him (the devil). It is the authority and the splendours of this world that will make men commit a serious sin. They will make a man tell lies on the pulpit; they will make a man turn his back on God. And it is for the splendours of this world that a man will kill his own son without thinking twice. The bible says,

> **⁹ People who want to get rich fall into temptation and a trap and into many foolish and harmful desires that plunge men into ruin and destruction.**
>
> **¹⁰ For the love of money is a root of all kinds of evil. Some people, eager for money, have wandered from the faith and pierced themselves with many griefs** *(I Timothy 6:9-10, NIV)*

This wave of prosperity gospel that started in the United States was blown by the wind across the ocean to Africa. This is where it made a mess. Given the poor status and poverty conditions of the continent, this new form of preaching became an opportunity for pastors to exploit the church. A lot of young pastors started to emerge. They claimed to be filled with the Holy Spirit, and they gave themselves titles. The first country in Africa that grabbed the wave of the prosperity gospel was Nigeria.

Once when I was in Venda an area in the north part of South Africa next to Zimbabwe, I encountered a pastor from Nigeria who called himself a prophet. After preaching his sermon, he told the congregation to pledge to God individually so that whatever amount of money a person pledged, God would double the portion. He started calling people who wanted to pledge 10,000 rand. Then he called people who wanted to pledge lesser amounts—all the way down to 1,000 rand. People stood up and started pledging thousands and thousands of rand. He did not go below 1,000 rand. He said those who pledged but who had not brought money with them to the church that day must bring it the following day. The following day the person who was collecting the money collected 13,000 rand from the few people who had been present at church that evening, and the pastor took the money away with him.

The most vulnerable group of people when it comes to quoted scripture, are Christians. People will not question or reason what is said by the person preaching, yet God says, **'Come now, let us reason together'** *(Isaiah 1:18).*

Nowhere in the scriptures does God require us to pledge money to Him. I was very angry with this man and the fact that he used the Bible and God for his devious ways of getting money from poor and vulnerable people. I later learned that the church where I fellowshipped was not the only church he had gotten money from. In some he got more than what he got from us. (By the way, my wife and I did not pledge.)

In South Africa this type of preaching of the gospel has created a huge problem with the youth. Young boys and girls are now moving to ministry at the early ages without any experience, commitment, or service to the church of God. In this country a lot of people from both within and from the outside are venturing into ministry because they see it as career not a calling. Most South Africans, because of the fear of God, tend to follow and listen to anybody who claims to be a man or woman of God or a pastor. Whatever that person says people will listen to without questioning the validity and the originality of the message. Pastors in this country want to live like kings with the money that comes from the people in the form of tithes. Pastors will preach about material things in the church more than the truth from the word of God.

I like Jim Reeves' song 'I'd Rather Have Jesus' when he says,

> I'd rather have Jesus than silver or gold.
> I'd rather be His than have riches untold.
> I'd rather have Jesus than houses or land.
> I'd rather have Jesus than worldly applause.

How I wish these words could be spoken by the pastors of today. What Jim Reeves is singing about is in the Bible: **'But seek first the kingdom of God and His righteousness, and all these things shall be added to you'** *(Matthew 6:33)*.

In one church I attended, our pastor invited as a guest speaker a certain man who had a doctorate in theology. The man stepped to the pulpit and, without opening any scripture, started telling the congregation about tithing. He said a person who does not tithe is supposed to be expelled from the church because that person is robbing the pastor of his salary.

The fear of God amongst people in the churches is not there any longer. Greed has taken over from salvation in churches today specially amongst the pastors. The Bible warns us:

> **¹ But know this, that in the last days perilous times will come:**

> **² For men will be lovers of themselves, lovers of money, boasters, proud, blasphemers, disobedient to parents, unthankful, unholy,**

> **³ unloving, unforgiving, slanderous, without self-control,
> brutal, despisers of good, traitors, headstrong, haughty,
> lovers of pleasure rather than lovers of God**
> *(II Timothy 3: 1-2).*

This is exactly what is happening now. Pastors love themselves and they love money. There is a lot of boasting about the numbers of congregants in their churches. They talk about 'my people', and they live a very unholy life, loving themselves rather than loving God. The phrases 'my people' and 'my church' are very common worldwide. Pastors are shepherds, and as shepherds they have a responsibility to look after God's flock not their own.

This is what Peter says to the pastors:

> **¹ To the elders among you, I appeal as a fellow elder, a
> witness of Christ's suffering and one who also will share
> in the glory to be revealed:**

> **² Be shepherds of God's flock that is under your care,
> serving as an overseers, not because you must, but because
> you are willing, as God wants you to be; not greedy for
> money, but eager to serve;**

> **³ not lording it over those entrusted to you, but being
> examples to the flock** *(I Peter 5: 1-3, NIV).*

Pastors should heed this call from Peter: they should be shepherds of God's flock not their own. People are not anybody's subjects but God's. When a call is from God rather than through a personal career choice, then that pastor will know that he or she is there to serve as an overseer who is willing to do God's will rather than follow personal goals. These pastors will be like the pastors of old, who were willing to do anything for God for little pay and without an accumulation of material wealth gleaned from the flock. The reward of being an example to the flock and obeying what Peter was talking about is: **'And when the Chief Shepherd appears, you will receive the crown of glory that will never fade away'** *(I Peter 5: 4, NIV).*

Pastors who do not take care of the flock that God has given them will be heavily punished by God. As shepherds of the flock, pastors are supposed to feed the sheep and look after the well-being of the flock, not the other way round. In cities, churches that don't have large congregations and don't receive generous tithes are closing down. Pastors are abandoning these churches, because they are unable to generate the amount of income that the pastor is looking for. In the book of Ezekiel, chapter 34, God warns the shepherds against feeding themselves and not the sheep.

I am not saying that pastors should not be paid for the work that they do; I am saying they should be paid according to the level of what their congregations can afford and to the level of what they are doing. Anybody who does any work for the church should be paid by the church unless the work is established ahead of time as voluntary work.

Pastors should stop competing with the world with regard to material things, because this is done at the expense of their congregations.

My Church, My People

As I have said, 'my church' and 'my people' are now very common phrases spoken by pastors when they refer to the church and the congregations nowadays. Jesus Christ said to Peter, **'And I also say to you that you are Peter, and on this rock I will build My church, and the gates of Hades shall not prevail against it'** *(Mathew 16: 18)*.

Jesus Christ never said that Peter would build his own church. The church belongs to Christ. It is His, not anybody else's. This is emphasised by Paul:

> **²⁵ For the husband is head of the wife, as also Christ is head of the church; and He is the Savior of the body.**
>
> **²⁴ Therefore, just as the church is subject to Christ, so let the wives be to their husbands in everything**
> *(Ephesians 5: 23-24)*.

Christ is the head of the church, and the church is subject to Him and nobody else. If I remember correctly, He is still the head of the church, and He has not abdicated that responsibility yet. All the members of the congregation belong to the body, which is the church, and that body is Christ's body: **'I now rejoice in my sufferings for you, and fill up in my flesh what is lacking in the afflictions of Christ, for the sake of His body, which is the church'** *(Colossians 1:24)*.

Jesus prayed for His disciples:

> **⁶ "I have revealed you to those whom you gave me out of the world. They were yours; you gave them to me and they have obeyed your word.**
>
> **⁷ Now they know that everything you have given me comes from you.**
>
> **⁸ For I gave them the words you have given me and they accepted them. They knew with certainty that I came from you, and they believe that you sent me.**
>
> **⁹ I pray for them. I am not praying for the world, but for those you have given me, for they are yours**
> *(John 17: 6-9, NIV).*

Jesus spent three years with the disciples, and yet there is not a single incident whereby He referred to them as 'my disciples.' He says, '**I have revealed you to those whom you gave me. They were yours; you gave them to me. I am not praying for the world, but for those you have given me, for they are yours**' *(John 17: 6-9).*

'**If My people who are called by My name . . .**' (II Chronicles 7:14). This is God speaking. No pastor 'has' people. All humans are God's creation, and He is the only one who can claim them. Some pastors make themselves gods. People have to stand when they walk in and out of church; in some cases people kneel down and bow to their pastors, and the pastors do not put a stop to this, as they love it. The Bible says one should not bow down to any gods except to the only true living God. Pastors are misleading the flock of God to satisfy their own desires and ambitions. Some hide behind culture. When a person is the child of the living God, there is only one culture—it is God's culture, and nothing else. The flock in the church belongs to God and has been bought by the blood of the Lamb.

> **'Therefore take heed to yourselves and to all the flock, among which the Holy Spirit has made you overseers, to shepherd the church of God which He purchased with His own blood'** *(Acts 20: 28).*

Pastors are called to shepherd the church of God. The Holy Spirit has made them overseers; they do not own the church or the people as possessions. Christ died for the church that some pastors call their own. He was crucified for the flock that they call 'my people'. What is happening nowadays in the African soil is directly opposite to what Paul said: **'I have never coveted anyone's silver or gold or fine clothes. You know that these hands of mine have worked to supply my own needs and the needs of those who were with me'** *(Acts 20: 33, NLT).*

This cannot be said by African pastors and ministers, as some of them go out of their way to please those who have silver and gold. This they do at the expense of poor people in the church. These days, the type of clothes you wear and the type of car you drive determine your seat in the church—not only your seat but also your role in the church and also your association with the pastor and the elders of the church. A man or a woman who carries silver and gold in churches today can commit sin in any way, but the pastor will never call them to order, and this is because the pastor is afraid they will leave the church with their tithe. In one church that I attended the pastor called everybody who had a service contract or wanted a service contract with the government to come forward for prayers.

There is a great competition among pastors regarding what car they drive, the labels of the clothes they wear, and the houses they build.

Personal Possession

Large congregations are a key issue in both city and town churches of late. If the church gathering has few congregants and it does not grow, it ceases to be a church. **'For where two or three are gathered together in My name, I am there in the midst of them'** *(Matthew 18:20)*. To God, the numbers are not an issue. As long as a gathering is about His name, He will show up and supply all the *needs*—not the *wants*—of that gathering. The reason that pastors and ministers want to grow their churches in huge numbers is all about their egos, and the fact that the huge numbers mean more money for them to satisfy their own personal wants.

In the church I attended, the pastor told the congregation that the church belonged to him and his family. 'We started this church as seven members of the family. It belongs to me and my family. Nobody will take it away from me.' One pastor built an empire in the church grounds, and the church is registered under his name and his wife's name. All that is in that churchyard is built from the money that came from the congregation funds. He has a fleet of cars that were all bought through the church funds. He controls everything in the church. The church elders have no say in how the finances are being used.

'Furthermore King David said to all the assembly: "My son Solomon, whom alone God Has chosen, is young and inexperienced; and the work is great, because the temple is not for man but for the Lord

God"' *(I Chronicles 29:1).* What pastor has the right, then, to claim as his own the house that he has built with the resources from the people of God, and further to register it under his own family's name? I don't care how much a pastor contributes to the building of a church. It is not the pastor's. God has contributed a lot to make the pastor what he or she is, and yet He allows the pastor to do what he or she likes with that body. When a pastor builds a structure and tells the congregation that he is building a church, he must know that is not his. It is the house of God. David took all that God had given to him and dedicated it to the building of the house of the Lord God.

> **² Now for the house of my God I have prepared with all my might: gold for things to be made of gold, silver for the things of silver, bronze for the things of bronze, iron for the things of iron, wood for the things of wood, onyx stones, stones to be set, glistening stones of various colors, and all kinds of precious stones and marble slabs in abundance.**
>
> **³ Moreover, because I have set my affection on the house of my God, I have given to the house of my God, over and above all that I have prepared for the holy house, my own special treasure of gold and silver: three thousand talents of gold, of the gold of Ophir, and seven thousands of refined silver, to overlay the walls of the house** *(I Chronicles 29:2-3).*

David did not spare the treasures he had collected during his period as the king. He even took what was his own personal treasure to build a house he called the house of God. Nowhere in the Bible did David refer to the house that he gave so much to it as 'my house and my family.' David never forced anybody to give towards the building of this house he called the house of God. After announcing to the assembly what he was going to give as the king:

> **⁶ Then the leaders of the fathers' house, leaders of the tribes of Israel, the captains of thousands and hundreds, with the officers' over the king's work, offered willingly.**

⁸ And whoever had precious stones gave them to treasury of the house of the Lord, into the hands of Jehiel the Gershonite.

⁹ Then the people rejoiced, for they had offered willingly, because with the loyal heart they had offered willingly to the Lord; and the king David also rejoiced greatly *(I Chronicles 29:6, 8, and 9).*

Jehiel was in charge of the treasuries of the house of God. People willingly gave the best they had towards the building of the house of the Lord. The money went into the treasury for the building of the house of the Lord. When people know that what they are doing is for the Lord—not for the pastor and his family—they will give freely and willingly with all their hearts, not with their minds. For they know that what they give is from God and is for God, so the amount is not an issue. The treasuries did not go to Zadok the priest or to Nathan the prophet.

One pastor I know of was very angry with the church he took over when the congregants were not giving him the offerings and tithes. He said to me 'These people—who do they think they are? I am the one who brings money by my preaching in the church, and yet they do not allow me to touch or to keep the money that I brought to the church! This is *my* church! I have a right to that money, not them.' I kept quiet because I was one of those who were responsible to bank the church money. The pastor who had served before this pastor never wanted to be involved with the church finances. He used to say to me 'Baba [which means 'daddy'. That's how he used to call me as his assistant pastor], I don't want to be involved with church money. My duty is to preach the word of God, and you must take care of all the other activities that are not related to spiritual issues, so that my attention is not disturbed by these small things.' He used to give a lot to the church from his business. Like David, he never referred to the church as *his*. He used to say, 'Baba, people must give to God willing without being manipulated into giving.'

In South Africa pastors are desperate for earthly wealth. With the new government and the service contract system that is all over the country, some pastors are into bidding for this government service contract work. There is nothing wrong with pastors bidding for this contract work, but in South Africa this bidding is closely associated with corruption. The bidding encourages bribery, manipulation, and backhand money. It is a known fact that the bidding system in this country leaves a lot to be desired. So the question is, why would a man of God be involved in such business? Love of money is the answer to this question. The love of money makes greedy Christians wander from the true faith, become liars, murderers, and sometimes end up as blasphemers. Pastors are honouring politicians in the church to beg for winning government contracts. Politicians are allowed by pastors to use the church as a platform for canvassing because they beg to be loved so that they can win these government contracts. The church is not a political platform; it is the house of God. I am not saying politicians should not go to church, but when they are in church they must be treated like all other congregants; they must not get special treatment and attention because they are politicians. The church has turned its back from God and it has become the lover of world possessions.

> **¹⁵ Do not love the world or anything in the world. If anyone loves the world, the love of the Father is not in him.**
>
> **¹⁶ For everything in the world-the cravings of sinful man, the lust of his eyes and the boasting of what he has and does—come not from God but from the world.**
>
> **¹⁷ The world and its desires pass away, but the man who does the will of God lives forever** (*I John 2:15-17, NIV*).

The Bible says, if you love the splendours and everything that glitters, then the love of God is surely not with you. You can't love God *and* money. One pastor was boasting in the church about his pair of suits that he bought for more than 20,000 rand.

'But now you boast in your arrogance. All such boasting is evil' (*James 4:16*). To boast about such things it is very arrogant especially that you bought them with the money that the church was supposed to use to feed the poor.

> **²³ This is what the Lord says:**
> **'Let not the wise man boast of his wisdom or the strong man boast of his strength or the rich man boast of his riches,**
>
> **²⁴ but let him who boasts boast about this: that he understands and knows me, that I am the Lord, who exercises kindness, justice and righteousness on earth, For in this I delight'** (*Jeremiah 9:23-24, NIV*).

God wants us to boast about Him, not about these things that are here today and gone tomorrow.

In South Africa, 20,000 rand can do a lot for an orphanage. What makes me sad is the fact that in my country we have a lot of orphanages and families that are headed by children, and they go to bed without food. African churches are doing very little to support these young people. Pastors want to wear expensive clothes and drive very expensive cars. It's not that they don't know about these poor people and orphanages. They know very well what they are supposed to do, but they choose to ignore it.

'Therefore, to him who knows to do good and does not do it, to him it is sin' (*James 4:17*). To ignore what you know you suppose to do and not do it is sin.

One day a black lady was featured on a television programme. She had elephantiasis on one of her legs. Her leg had become quite large, and the condition was threatening her life. The doctors could not operate due to her lack of finances. A white farmer donated money for the surgery. On a later episode of the same programme, they asked the farmer what made him donate towards the lady's operation. This is what he said: 'I had this money that was about 450,000 rand that I saved to buy equipment for my farm. When I saw this lady's leg and that she could not be operated on due to financial lack from her family, I realised that my farm equipment could wait for later, and the money could help the person whose life was threatened by death. A person cannot die because of lack of money.' It touched my heart that a farmer could forget about material things and think of saving a person's life.

> **'Pure and genuine religion in the sight of God the Father means caring for orphans and widows in their distress and refusing to let the world corrupt you'** *(James 1:27, NLT).*

But pastors would rather allow the world to corrupt them than heed this call.

Peter brought Tabitha back from death because of what the Bible described as doing good and helping the poor.

Called Alone

I talked about pastors making a church a family affair. I am talking about a man who claimed that the church actually belonged to him and his family. When God calls a man, he calls him alone—not his wife as well. There is a new trend in most ministries—a pastor will be the head of the church and his wife will be a co-pastor in the same church. There can be only one shepherd called by God for the flock. In these churches, if the pastor is not present, the wife takes over. When God gave instruction in the Garden of Eden, He gave instruction to Adam, not to Adam and Eve together. When God called Moses up in the mountain, He called him alone. God spoke to Abraham alone; the promise of the son was between God and Abraham. Jesus Christ, when He called His disciples, called them alone; I am sure some of these guys were married. When God calls a woman, He calls that woman alone.

'Now Deborah, a prophetess, the wife of Lapidoth, was judging Israel at that time' *(Judges 4:4)*. This is the only time Deborah's husband is mentioned in the portion of the Bible that mentions Deborah. There is no evidence that she consulted her husband about decisions she had to make; neither was her husband second in command in Israel when his wife was judging. God does not confuse issues. He will call a man or a woman. He will not call the husband and wife for the same job at the same time for the same church, for to God each and every one of us has a different calling. Marrying a pastor does not automatically makes one a pastor. There is not a single instance in the Bible in which God called a prophet and the prophet's wife became a prophet also. Marriage does not qualify a person to carry out the same responsibilities as his or her spouse. A president's wife does not become a president because her husband is a president; neither does a queen's husband become a king because he is married to a queen.

'After you put these clothes on your brother Aaron and his sons, anoint and ordain them. Consecrate them, so they may serve me as priests' *(Exodus 28:41, NIV)*. God did not say to Moses, 'Take Aaron your brother and his wife and anoint and ordain them.' God said 'his sons' so that Aaron's lineage would become the priesthood of Israel, which is going to serve God. So it was with Aaron's son, grandson, and great-grandson, and so on down the family line. Nowhere did one of the son's wives become priests.

In one church I attended both the husband and the wife were the pastors of the church, and they were both drawing a salary from the church. Everything that the wife did not like at the church also affected the husband. Things that the man could have solved as the pastor were dealt with in a very emotional way. In pastoral meetings, elders were very cautious and became afraid to say anything that might affect the wife or oppose her, for fear of the pastor's wrath. She was always present in the meetings. This compromised the freedom of expression in the church.

In one church the pastor told the congregation that they were going to embark on Daniel fasting for forty days. His wife preached few weeks afterwards, just before they started with fasting, and she told the congregation that there is nothing called Daniel fasting in the Bible. The day the husband was talking about the Daniel fasting the wife had been absent, and coincidentally or deliberately so, the wife contradicted her husband in absentia. Can you imagine what this does to the congregation when two pastors are saying two opposite things to the same congregation?

The reason that pastors favour making their wives pastors in the same church is to safeguard what they call 'my church' and 'my people' and all other assets of the church that are purchased through the church funds for the ministry of God. They don't want to lose what they see as what is for them, but not for God.

Healing School

When I was at high school way back 1975, I developed a pain in the lower part of my belly that used to knock me down. The pain occurred on and off. When I experienced the pain, I would have to sit down because I had difficulty walking. I went to a public hospital, and doctors did not know what it was. I stayed with this pain until I got married to Matshele. One day in 1993 it got me. My wife wanted to know what it was. I told her that it was my old sickness. Being a doctor, she was concerned. I told her that it was an old pain . . . it wouldn't kill me, and I would be fine. She didn't take it lightly, as I had. She called one of the best surgeons in Johannesburg and made an appointment. By the time I got to the surgeon, the pain was gone. He examined me and couldn't find anything, but he then decided to send me for ultrasound. The results came back negative. He sent me for a CT scan. The scan results came back negative. He said to me, 'Mr. Kewana, all the results are showing negative and I can't find anything wrong with you. I don't want to cut you for something I don't know. If it comes back and persists, please do come back then I will see what I can do.'

After this I said to myself, *There is nothing wrong with me. I should be fine.* Then one Saturday morning during my morning run, when I was far from home, the pain came back. I said to myself, *Lord not now, I am far from home and I am alone. What am I going to do with this pain?* A little voice reminded me of the scripture:

¹⁵ And He said to them, 'Go into the world and preach the gospel to every creature.

¹⁶ He who believes and is baptized will be saved; but he who does not believe will be condemned.

¹⁷ And these signs will follow those who believe: In My name they will cast out demons; they will speak with new tongues;

¹⁸ they will take up serpents; and if they drink anything deadly, it will by no means hurt them; they will lay hands on the sick, they will recover' *(Mark 16:15-18).*

I immediately said to myself, *Hey Thuso, you are the child of God. You believe in Jesus Christ, so why should you suffer with a pain that even doctors cannot find the cause of?* I put my hands where the pain was and I said, 'In the name of Jesus, pain be gone!' It didn't take a second! The pain was gone and I continued with my running. That was the last time I ever had that pain.

One day my wife was so very sick that she lay in bed. She had promised our little four-year-old daughter that she would take her to town. Our daughter asked her mom why she was still sleeping and if they were still going to town. My wife said they couldn't go because she was ill. Our daughter said, 'Mommy can I pray for you so that you can be better?' My wife said, 'Yes.' As a loving mother, she agreed to make her daughter feel happy. Our daughter laid her hands on her mother's forehead and said, 'Jesus, will you make my mummy better so that we can go to town? Amen.' There and then my wife recovered.

My little daughter knew that Jesus can heal people. When she was born she had problems with her ears. They use to ooze out puss. The ear, nose, and throat surgeon prevented her from swimming, and she loved water like all other children. Later on the doctor suggested earplugs. This did not help much as they would sometimes fall out when she was swimming. One day when she was three years old, we were at church and our daughter said to her mom that she was going to ask the pastor to pray for her ears. She walked to the front of the church all by herself and she spoke to the pastor. We saw the pastor putting his hands on her ears and praying. She came back and told her mother that her ears had been healed. From that day onwards she refused to use her earplugs, and her ears never oozed again.

A close friend of mine, who is a paediatrician, urgently called my wife to the hospital one day to explain to a mother in the Xhosa language about her boy, who had been involved in a car accident and had sustained head injuries. The boy was having seizures and had been given the drug Tegretol (carbamazepine) by the doctor. From that he developed Steven Johnson Syndrome, and the prognosis was poor. The boy did not look good; his eyes were affected, and he was admitted into the intensive care unit. The doctor said the boy might not survive, and if he did survive, he would be just a cabbage with a brain that was dead. I was with my wife in the ICU as the doctor was explaining all these things to my wife, who is also a doctor. The three of us—my wife, the doctor, and I—decided to pray for the boy. The doctor was my friend, and I knew he was a dedicated Christian.

The following day we came back and prayed again. Within a week the boy was transferred out of intensive care into a general ward. The second week he was discharged, walking and talking just like all the other children. The boy's mother was from Mpumalanga and she and her son returned there. After a year she came to visit in Cape Town. With her was a young man who was very active. She came to tell us this was the boy who had been involved in the accident. God had healed that boy from whatever damage had occurred in his body. No man has healing powers; only God does. God gives to whoever believes in His Son.

Did my wife, my daughter, or I go to a healing school in order to heal or be healed? No. Jesus Christ said, '**And these signs will follow those who believe ... In My name they shall lay hands on the sick, and they will recover**' *(Mark 16:17 and 18)*. He never said that the sick must graduate from a healing school before they recover; neither did he say that the healing powers are given to certain people. Did He say that it would be certain churches, or certain pastors who could heal? No. These signs will follow those who believe, and in His name they shall. It means anyone who believes is capable of laying hands on the sick and they will recover in the name of Jesus. It is not a healing school that heals people, but it is the name of Jesus. This has been given to all those who believe in Him. Healing schools are a money-making schemes. They are not scriptural.

According to Paul, healing is a gift from the Spirit: **To another faith by the same Spirit, to another gifts of healing by the same Spirit'** *(I Corinthians 12:9)*. Further along in the chapter he says, **'And God has appointed these in the church: first apostles, second prophets, third teachers, after that miracles, then gifts of healing, helps, administrations, varieties of tongues'** *(I Corinthians 12:28)*.

People with healing gifts are there in your church. Pastors who do not have healing gifts must give way to other people to exercise what God has given them in the church. Healing is a gift, and nobody pays for a gift. It is a free gift from God. **'Heal the sick, cleanse the lepers, raise the dead, cast out demons. Freely you have received, freely give'** *(Matthew 10:8)*.

In the Bible story, the woman who had a bleeding problem was healed by touching Jesus's garment. Jesus never demanded a proof of her sickness from all the physicians she had attended before she received her healing. When the centurion came to Jesus and pleaded with Him to heal his servant who was lying at home paralyzed and in pain, Jesus did not request proof from the doctor to confirm the servant's sickness. It seems wrong to me that today people should bring a proof from the doctor about their sickness. Healing should not be done by the pastors to please the world. If we know that it is God who heals, and not a person, we don't have to provide proof to anybody for what God has done.

I have said this, and I am going to keep on saying it again and again— the flock is very vulnerable, and true shepherds are sensitive to that vulnerability. But those who are hired to look after the flock will not care about this vulnerability, and so they will cause harm as they exploit the vulnerability for their own gain. God will not judge the flock, but He will judge the shepherds heavily. The shepherds don't teach the flock the truth about the word of God; instead they tell them lies and manipulate the flock's emotions for their own benefit. There is no compassion amongst these pastors towards the people of God. As the true shepherd, Christ was driven by compassion every time He saw the flock. He did something for flock; he did not expect the flock to do something for Him.

There are so-called great ministers of God, who move around the world. Strangely enough, when they come to Africa, there are only two countries they will visit—Nigeria and South Africa. The African ministers will always visit one country in Africa, and that is South Africa. The reason for this is that South Africans have money. These ministers have never been to Malawi, Zimbabwe, Zambia, Swaziland, and all these small and poor African countries.

If these African ministers go overseas, they chose United States of America, the United Kingdom, Canada, Germany, and other rich European countries. They won't go to the small poor Eastern countries where the gospel is really needed most. Then the question is this: Is it all about preaching the gospel to the poor or is about impressing those who have money?

Bible Study

I tried to study theology, but I dropped out of three different colleges. I would register and start studying. On the first test I would get very good grades—not less than 80 percent. Strangely enough, I wouldn't go far, and my spirit would feel uneasy. This would make me stop there and then. I guess God did not want me to get this revelation through any man; rather he wanted me to receive the teachings from the Holy Spirit: **'But the Helper, the Holy Spirit, whom the Father will send in My name, He will teach you all things, and bring to your remembrance all things that I said to you'** *(John 14:26)*.

Christ is saying here that the Holy Spirit will teach us all things about Him. I don't hear Him commanding His disciples to go and start bible schools to teach people the word of God. After healing the crippled beggar, Peter and John started addressing the people who were in the temple: **'Now when they saw the boldness of Peter and John, and perceived that they were uneducated and untrained men, they marveled. And they realized that they had been with Jesus'** *(Acts 4:13)*.

It is God who gives knowledge and wisdom. Knowing God and His son Jesus Christ is the foundation of all things. All the hidden treasures of the heavenly kingdom are revealed to those who seek Him diligently. **'In whom are hidden all the treasures of wisdom and knowledge'** *(Colossians 2:3)*. The Bible is the word of God not of man. If we seek God first, all other things will be revealed to us by the Holy Spirit. What surprises me is that in one city you can find more than four different churches depending on the size of the city, each and every one with its own Bible study with totally different teaching materials that supposedly refer to the same Bible. Paul, in the book of **Galatians, says,**

> [11] **But I make known to you, brethren, that the gospel which was preached by me is not according to man.**

> [12] **For I neither received it from man, nor was I taught it, but it came through the revelation of Jesus Christ'** *(Galatians 1:11-12).*

Here is a man who wrote almost half on the New Testament saying that whatever he wrote did not come from any man, but from Christ Himself. Let Christ, through the Holy Spirit, be only one to reveal the scriptures to you. God says, **'Then I will give them a heart to know Me, that I am the Lord; and they shall be My people, I will be their God, for they shall return to Me with their whole heart'** *(Jeremiah 24: 7).*

God will give us a heart to know Him—nobody else can do that.

God as an Employer

When God calls a man to work for Him, God provides. God never calls a man and does not provide for all the needs that the man will require to carry out His work. He will never make a man a beggar after He has called him. What I am talking about is evident right through the whole Bible, but for the sake of time and space I don't want to rewrite the Bible in this book. I will quote a few examples from the scriptures. I am doing this just to show that God, like all other employers, cares about those who are truly employed by Him—not the self-appointed ones who claim to be working for Him.

God called Moses from shepherding sheep and sent him to Egypt to liberate the Israelites from slavery. When Moses arrived in Egypt, he found that the Israelites were slaves; they had nothing except for flocks and herds—no gold or silver . . . no precious stones or clothing. However, when Israelites left Egypt, they had great possessions.

> **35 Now the children of Israel had done according to the word of Moses, and they had asked from the Egyptians articles of silver, articles of gold, and clothing.**
>
> **36 And the Lord had given the people the favor in the sight of Egyptians, so they granted them what they requested. Thus they plundered the Egyptians** (*Exodus 12:35-36*).

This plundering of the Egyptians by the Israelites is not something that happened by chance or on the spur of the moment:

> **15 God said to Abram 'Knowing certainly that your descendants will be strangers in a land that is not theirs, and will serve them, and they will afflict them four hundred years.**
>
> **14 And also the nation whom they will serve I will judge; afterward they shall come out with great possessions'** *(Genesis 15:13-14).*

God will always provide for His children no matter what. During the Israelites' journey, God provided for their every need. Moses never approached any of the nations on his journey and asked them to donate or give to the Israelites. Every time they wanted something, Moses went to the Lord, and God provided.

Jesus took twelve men who were working different jobs and providing for their families, and gave them different employment, which did not provide them with any materialistic remuneration. If my memory serves me well, I don't remember reading about them or Jesus asking for donations or asking people to support them financially in Jesus's ministry so that they could receive double blessings. What is stranger, they were able to feed the poor out of nothing. Christ provided not only for the poor but for the disciples as well. They walked with Jesus for kilometres on foot for three years. When Jesus was confronted by the rich young man about inheriting the kingdom of heaven, Jesus did not lecture about the rich man tithing to His ministry, or giving to the kingdom of heaven. He preached about the rich man giving to the poor.

When the angel of the Lord sent Philip to talk to the Ethiopian man who was in charge of all the Ethiopian queen's treasury, he did not talk to him about tithing, giving to the ministry or to the kingdom. Surely this was not a poor man. But this is the kind of preaching that is common in churches these days—people are advised to give money to the church.

If a person is called by God to the ministry, surely God will provide for that person. When a pastor called by God to do God's work asks for donations from other people, he is saying that his employer, who is God, cannot meeting his needs for the ministry. This then makes God a very bad employer—one who calls people to the ministry and then fails to provide for them to further the kingdom of heaven. What is strange with African pastors is that they ask for donations in US dollars, British pounds, or euros, and never in their local currency.

Fashion Show

hat I am going to talk about here is nicely covered in The Message, a contemporary language translation of the Bible that is not divided into traditional verses. The scripture reads as follows: '**They love to sit at the head table at church dinners, basking in the most prominent positions, preening in the radiance of public flattery, receiving honorary degrees, and getting called "Doctor" and "Reverend"'** *(Matthew 23, MSG).*

It is strange that something that Jesus Christ warned His disciples and other people about two thousand years ago is still happening to the pastors in this era. They love front seats when they visit other church services, funerals, or any church function. They love to be introduced with their titles of pastor, prophet, bishop, or doctor.

In South Africa, pastors are buying honorary doctorates like sweets. It is not surprising in South Africa to hear a pastor introduced as 'Doctor Bishop So & So' or 'Doctor Prophet So & So'. Pastors want to identify themselves with the world. They want to be accepted as one who holds a worldly title. They would rather be recognized by their worldly title than the one the church gives them.

To the world, it's more honourable to be referred to as a pastor than as a doctor. Strangely enough, to our pastors it is more honourable to be recognized and referred to by the worldly title of honorary doctorate.

Some of our honoured bishops in this country have honorary doctorates, but, in all humility, they have not allowed people to address them as 'doctor'. They have worked hard to earn those honorary doctorates. One thing for sure is that people cannot use a person's title if they do not know it. Or if they do know it and are asked not to use it, they will respect that wish. The issue of titles in South Africa is like a fashion show. Titles will not take anybody to Heavenly Paradise. For some strange reason this sickness of titles is common with so-called Pentecostal or Charismatic churches. These are the people who claim to be filled with the Holy Spirit, and yet they are obsessed with worldly recognition.

Conclusion

Jesus took business people as his disciples. These were men who had their own businesses. Matthew, the tax collector, was very rich in those days. Jesus took them away from their worldly material possessions and made them follow him for three years, during which time he taught them the true gospel. These men left all their earthly wealth and followed Jesus. And, after His ascension, they continued with the gospel and most of them were martyred for their beliefs.

Jesus never ordered them to start their own church and gather huge numbers of followers and call them 'their own'. He never taught them how to preach a tithing gospel. He ordered them to make disciples out of the people they preached to, not congregants who would tithe to them so that they could flourish and be wealthy. In this world nowadays a man will come from nowhere as poor as a church mouse, call himself a pastor, and start a church. Within few years, he will become very rich with worldly materials all gained from the congregants' tithes.

The truth of the word of God is in the Bible; it does not come from the mouths of pastors. I urge everybody to read the word of God and ask the Holy Spirit for revelation and the understanding of the word. God is not a respecter of any men, but only of those who follow His principles.

I pray that the Holy Spirit will reveal the truth as it is from the word of God—the Holy Bible. And I pray that you will find courage to read the word of God every day of your life so as to get guidance from Him.

May the true living God our Father, His son Jesus Christ, and the Holy Spirit be with you all the days of your life.